The Easter Rising

At midday on Easter Monday, April 24, 1916, a pale-faced man in a green uniform stood on the steps of the General Post Office in Dublin and read out to a small and bewildered crowd the proclamation of the Irish republic. He was Patrick Henry Pearse, and his words signaled the beginning of a nationalist rebellion against British rule.

The British authorities were taken by surprise, but despite the demands of World War I (then in its second year) they were able to summon enough soldiers and guns to crush the Rising within a week. Over four hundred people were killed, some of the most beautiful parts of Dublin were destroyed, and the leaders of the Rising were shot as traitors a few days later.

Pearse and his associates knew that by signing the proclamation they were signing away their lives. Their purpose was to administer a shock to the Irish people — to show that the British government was autocratic and oppressive, and to kindle the spark of militant nationalism into an unquenchable blaze. Although the Rising seemed, on the face of it, a disastrous failure, its leaders' purpose was achieved. It destroyed the entire basis on which, in the past, Irishmen had negotiated with the British for greater independence, and it pointed to the end of seven centuries of British dominance over Ireland.

LIST OF IMPORTANT
IRISH ORGANIZATIONS

FIANNA, a youth movement founded in 1909 by Bulmer Hobson and Countess Markievicz.

GAELIC ATHLETIC ASSOCIATION, founded in 1884.

GAELIC LEAGUE, a movement for the revival of the Irish language, history, and culture, founded in 1893 by MacNeill and others.

IRISH CITIZEN ARMY, militant nationalist force of trade unionists founded by Connolly and Larkin in 1913.

IRISH OR HOME RULE PARTY, the majority of the Irish members of the British House of Commons, led first by Charles Parnell and later by John Redmond.

IRISH REPUBLICAN BROTHERHOOD, a secret society founded in 1858 that aimed to establish an Irish republic, by force if necessary.

IRISH VOLUNTEERS, founded in 1913 in response to the Ulster Volunteers by MacNeill, Pearse, and others; in effect, an unofficial Irish army.

SINN FEIN ("Ourselves"), nationalist political movement founded in early 1900's and led by Arthur Griffith, which aimed at complete independence through a policy of noncooperation with the British.

PRINCIPALS

The signers of the proclamation of the Irish republic:

PATRICK (PADRAIC) H. PEARSE, teacher, poet, provisional president of the republic.

JAMES CONNOLLY, labor leader and leader of the Irish Citizen Army, commandant of the Dublin forces.

THOMAS J. CLARKE, Fenian revolutionary and IRB leader.

SEAN MacDERMOTT (MAC DIARMADA), Irish Republican Brotherhood organizer.

JOSEPH PLUNKETT, director of military operations, Irish Volunteers.

THOMAS MacDONAGH, director of training, Irish Volunteers.

EAMONN CEANNT (KENT), founder member of the Volunteers.

EOIN (JOHN) MacNEILL, university professor and head of the Irish Volunteers.

SIR ROGER CASEMENT, former British official and Irish nationalist.

ARTHUR GRIFFITH, Sinn Fein leader.

JOHN REDMOND, leader of the Irish Home Rule party in Parliament.

AUGUSTINE BIRRELL, chief secretary for Ireland.

SIR MATTHEW NATHAN, undersecretary for Ireland.

SIR EDWARD CARSON, Ulster Unionist leader.

MAJOR GENERAL SIR JOHN MAXWELL, British commander-in-chief in Ireland.

THE EASTER RISING

Dublin 1916
The Irish Rebel
Against British Rule

By Neil Grant

A World Focus Book

FRANKLIN WATTS, INC.
NEW YORK, 1972

Cover design by Nick Krenitsky
Maps by George Buctel

Library of Congress Cataloging in Publication Data

Grant, Neil.
 The Easter Rising, Dublin, 1916.

 (A world focus book)
 SUMMARY: An account of the events and prin-
cipals that precipitated the Easter Rising in Dublin and
the rebellion's influence on British rule in Ireland.
 Bibliography: p.
 1. Ireland–History–Sinn Fein Rebellion, 1916–Ju-
venile literature. [1. Ireland–History–Sinn Fein Rebellion, 1916] I. Title.
DA962.G68   941.59   72-3532
ISBN 0-531-02161-0

Contents

N

ATLANTIC

OCEAN

S C O T L A N D

ST. PATRICK'S (NORTH) CHANNEL

Larne

Lough
Neagh

Belfast

U L S T E R

Donegal Bay

Lough
Erne

Sligo

ISLE OF MAN

U N I T E D

Dundalk
Bay

IRISH   SEA

Lough
Mask

Lough Ree

C O N N A U G H T

K I N G D O M

Lough
Corrib

Galway

Dublin   Howth

Galway Bay

Liffey River

ARAN
ISLS.

L E I N S T E R

Lough
Derg

Shannon

Limerick

River

M U N S T E R

Tralee Bay

Suir R.

Barrow R.

ST. GEORGE'S (SOUTH) CHANNEL

W A L E S

E N G L A N D

Waterford

Lakes of
Killarney

Blackwater   R.

Cork

I   R   E   L   A   N   D

**IRELAND
1916**

0   25   50   75   100

Miles

ENGLISH CHANNEL

"The Irish Question"

Critics of Great Britain during the late nineteenth century liked to reveal the paradox of a country that claimed a vast world empire yet could not govern an island on its own doorstep. Ireland — poor, resentful, and rebellious — lay a few uncomfortable hours across the Irish Sea, a perpetual thorn in Britain's side. In one form or another, "the Irish Question" cropped up to trouble succeeding governments as it had, off and on, since the Middle Ages.

Someone complained that every time Britain tried to settle "the Irish Question," the Irish changed the question, but whatever the succession of puzzled British ministers might feel, the fundamental question was straightforward: Ireland wanted self-government. In particular, it wanted to repeal the Act of Union of 1800, which had merged Ireland with Great Britain and abolished the Irish Parliament in exchange for Irish representation in the British House of Commons.

In Ireland, however, nothing is ever as simple as it seems, and to portray Ireland as an oppressed colonial community united in seeking independence from its masters is to paint an oversimplified and distorted picture. The divisions within Ireland itself were as sharp and as numerous as the divisions between Ireland and Great Britain.

Those who could not pay the rent were thrown out of their cottages. The rough tripod supports a battering ram, to smash the walls and make the cottage uninhabitable. Some of the men carry makeshift shields to guard against buckets of hot water thrown by the occupants.

Who Owns Ireland?

Except in the region of Belfast, and on a smaller scale in Dublin, there was virtually no industry in nineteenth-century Ireland. The great mass of the population lived on the land as tenant farmers, many of them scratching a living from five or ten acres. Nearly all of the land was owned by a small class of Anglo-Irish gentry — "the Ascendancy" — who usually lived in England or elsewhere, leaving their estates in the hands of managers.

The precarious living of the Irish peasants collapsed completely in 1845–49, the years of the famine, when the potato crop (the staple — indeed the *only* — food of many people) failed several years running. Even in Ireland's disaster-ridden history, the horrors of the famine stand out grimly. The British government was incapable of dealing with the crisis, and with no food and no money, thousands of people were faced with a simple choice: get out or starve. The population of Ireland, which had been growing until 1845, was then about 8.5 million; by 1851 it was 6.5 million. In six desperate years nearly one-quarter of the inhabitants had vanished. Some had died, others had emigrated to England or, more and more, to North America. The trickle of Irish emigrants to the New World suddenly became a flood, which continued fairly steadily for the next three generations. Between 1841 and 1925, over 5 million Irish people entered the United States or Canada.

For twenty years after the famine, Ireland escaped a major crisis, but the 1870's brought bad times again. Some reforms were at last being made, however. Fewer people were living on the fringe of starvation, and there were more small farmers who at least owned the land they lived on and could no longer be turned

5

out of their homes according to the landlord's whim. Yet many were still evicted for nonpayment of rent— about a thousand families in 1879 alone. That was a terrible year; one that witnessed new outbreaks of violence (including murder), "land-grabbing" (illegal seizing of vacant farms), and starvation. From this time too dates the practice of the boycott — refusing all contact with anyone who had offended the community.

The British government, then headed by the great Liberal leader, W. E. Gladstone, attempted to deal with the worsening land problem by an act of Parliament, passed in 1881, that was designed to give some security to tenants. It was neither the first nor the last Irish land act, and although it brought improvements, it did not solve the basic problem.

New land acts were passed during the 1880's and 1890's, which allowed more tenant farmers to buy their land with money lent by the government, and various schemes of reform were introduced by nongovernment agencies. Some enlightened landowners, like Sir Horace Plunkett and Lord Monteagle, began a system of agricultural cooperatives, and an Irish department of agriculture was established. Violence in the countryside dwindled, and the 1903 land act speeded up the transfer of land from the great landowners to the farmers. It seemed that the long "war" between landowner and tenant might end peacefully.

The question of land ownership, a simple enough economic question, had always seemed to be at the bottom of Ireland's problems. If the question had been only an economic one it might have been solved, but economic questions can never be entirely separated from political or religious questions — especially not in Ireland. The slow process of government reforms and the well-meant attempts at compromise by moderate men on both sides were not enough to unite Ireland's deep divisions.

Home Rule

The people of nineteenth-century Ireland, like the people of England, were represented by members of Parliament meeting in London. Out of a total of approximately six hundred seats in the House of Commons, about one hundred went to Irish members.

From about 1870 onward, there were two main parties in Parliament: the Conservatives under Benjamin Disraeli (Lord Beaconsfield) and the Liberals under William Ewart Gladstone. Irish members formed a third party, which, under the leadership of one of the most brilliant politicians of the age, Charles Parnell, became a force to be reckoned with. The Irish party generally numbered about seventy (numbers went up or down slightly at each election). The remaining thirty-odd Irish members, chiefly from the province of Ulster, did not belong because they opposed the overriding aim of the Irish party — home rule for Ireland.

The battle for home rule was the greatest domestic political issue in Great Britain during the second half of the nineteenth century. But what exactly did "home rule" mean? It was not always possible to say. Of course it meant self-government for Ireland, but it did not mean complete independence. Parnell (a Protestant, incidentally) and his colleagues did not wish complete separation from Britain, and they were generally reluctant to spell out exactly the degree of independence they required. They acknowledged that matters of foreign policy, for example, would have to remain under some form of British control; they did not care to rid themselves of the British monarchy; and they did not demand an Irish republic. Thus they were not in sympathy with the Irish Republican Brotherhood (IRB), the secret society that was behind the unsuccessful revolt of 1867.

As the Irish party was vastly outnumbered by both Conser-

7

vatives and Liberals, it may seem surprising that it was able to accomplish anything at all in Parliament. However, the two main parties were sometimes very evenly balanced, and the Irish party could extract concessions from one or the other by promising (or withholding) its support.

A great moment for the Irish party came in 1885, when the Liberal prime minister, Gladstone, announced his conversion to home rule and prepared to bring a home rule bill before Parliament. Influenced by Parnell, Gladstone had been moving toward this decision for several years, but it was still an act of great political courage, for it split his party in two and provoked a furious storm of opposition.

The bill was defeated and Gladstone's government fell as a result, but from this time onward the Liberal party, though seriously weakened by the crisis, favored the principle of Irish home rule.

A few years later Parnell was involved in a scandal concerning his relationship with the wife of another member of Parliament; he fell from power and died soon afterward. The scandal split the Irish party no less effectively than home rule had split the Liberals, and it was not reunited until 1900. Meanwhile, Gladstone, back in power, resolutely introduced a second home rule bill in 1893. This time it passed the House of Commons but was defeated in the upper house (the House of Lords), which was generally more conservative than the Commons.

When the Irish party was reunited in 1900, John Redmond became its chairman. Redmond was to end his career in failure,

John Redmond — caricature of the Irish Home Rule leader, by "Spy."

with his life's work in shreds, but he was a more effective and more skillful politician than he later seemed. Moderate but firm, intelligent, honest, and a good speaker, he was a particularly good man to unite the party. Like Parnell before him, he was a well-to-do country gentleman (the members of the Irish party nearly all belonged to the prosperous, but small, middle class), but unlike Parnell, Redmond loved Britain and the British. He felt thoroughly at home in Parliament, where Parnell, while operating with equal skill, had always felt a stranger. It was Redmond's loyalty to Britain that led him into a serious error when the British empire seemed threatened by the outbreak of World War I.

In the election of 1905, the Liberal party in Britain won a surprising landslide victory. The prospects for home rule looked good — or did they?

Enjoying such a large majority in the House of Commons, the Liberal government did not depend on Irish votes for its survival, and it soon became clear that Gladstone's successors were in no special hurry to reopen the tricky question of Irish home rule. In 1909, however, the government became involved in a crisis that had nothing to do with Ireland. Not for the first time, the Conservative majority in the House of Lords brought the Liberal government to a halt by refusing to pass government acts. The constitutional upheaval that followed had two important results for the Irish party. In the first place, the power of the Lords was severely curbed: in the future, they would be able to delay, but not block, government acts. This removed one obstacle to home rule. In the second place, as a result of new elections, the Liberals lost their large majority in the House of Commons. In fact the balance between Liberals and Conservatives (who had, incidentally, taken the name Unionists as a sign of their opposition to home rule) was exactly even — 272 members each. The young Labor party had 42 seats, and Redmond's Irish Home Rulers had 73.

Redmond was thus in the happy position of controlling the balance of power in the House of Commons. Because the Liberal government needed his support, it became inevitable that the government would have to tackle home rule. Accordingly, the third home rule bill was introduced into the House of Commons in 1912 and subsequently passed. But it never went into effect because the outbreak of World War I caused its postponement. And by the time the war ended, home rule was dead.

"Ulster will fight..."

Britain became a Protestant country during the sixteenth century, while Ireland remained Roman Catholic. Thus, very few Irishmen belonged to the established, Protestant Church of Ireland and, as Catholics, the Irish were denied many civil rights until the Catholic Emancipation Act of 1829. Even after that, Catholics did not enjoy full equality; for example, there was no Catholic university in Ireland until 1908. Not everyone in Ireland was a Catholic, of course. In 1901, Catholics accounted for about three-quarters of the population, and of the Protestant remainder, only about half belonged to the dominant Anglican Church.

This division in religion paralleled the division in wealth and power — the poor were generally Catholics and the wealthy were generally Protestants. Government, the law, and education were dominated by Protestants, the descendants mainly of English settlers who had been sent to Ireland generations earlier to keep the country in order. To give just one example: out of eighteen High Court judges in Ireland, only three were Catholics.

Protestantism was strongest in the northeastern province of Ulster, especially in the six counties of Ulster that today form Northern Ireland. In that region there were more Protestants than Catholics. There too were concentrated almost all of Ireland's heavy industry: ship-building, engineering, and linen manufacture; and there was the center of Ireland's export trade. To maintain that trade and the industry behind it, the British market was essential. An independent Ireland, with its own protective trade tariffs, would destroy the special advantages that Ulster industry enjoyed as a result of the union with Britain.

Ulstermen therefore had many reasons for resisting home

Workers leaving Harland and Wolff shipyards in Belfast — then and now one of the chief employers in Ireland and a comparatively rare example of major industry. The ship under construction in the background is the Titanic, *the largest liner ever built, which sank on her maiden voyage in 1912.*

In Belfast City Hall, a grim-faced Carson signs the Ulster Covenant "to defeat the present conspiracy to set up a Home Rule Parliament in Ireland," September 1912.

rule. Their religion ("Home Rule means Rome Rule!" cried the Ulster Protestants, fearful of the power of the Roman Catholic Church), their political dominance, and their prosperity would all be imperiled by an independent Ireland. When Gladstone introduced his first home rule bill, Lord Randolph Churchill, then the champion of the Ulster Unionists, delivered his notorious warning: "Ulster will fight, and Ulster will be right!"

Ireland is a country where paradoxes flourish like weeds, yet the prospect of Irishmen fighting a civil war in order to remain a part of the country they were fighting against was a strange one, even for Ireland. Strange or not, so fierce was the opposition to home rule in Ulster that Lord Randolph's prophecy did not seem unlikely.

In 1910, when the constitutional crisis over the House of Lords was blowing up, the Ulster Unionists (Conservatives) elected Sir Edward Carson as their leader. Born in Dublin (not all Irish Unionists came from Ulster), Carson was an Anglo-Irishman who had made a great reputation as a criminal lawyer (he was the prosecuting attorney at the trial of Oscar Wilde). Tall, powerful, and grim, Carson was a vivid speaker and a courageous politician. On behalf of Ulster, he declared implacable opposition to the idea of home rule for Ireland, and prepared a "provisional government" of Ulster to take over when home rule went into effect.

On the other side, John Redmond and his colleagues were not willing to purchase home rule at the cost of splitting Ireland in two. Geographically, Ireland was obviously one country, and before 1916 few men on either side would accept the prospect — now the fact — of two Irelands. Compromise seemed impossible.

The Revolutionary Tradition

The Irish parliamentary party reflected with rough accuracy the desires of the majority of the Irish people who were opposed to the union. But there had always been a minority who had no use for constitutional methods or moderate policies and wanted an independent Irish state completely separate from Britain. To gain that end, they were willing to use any methods.

Until after the Easter Rising, the number of those willing to resort to war was always small, despite the endemic violence between landlord and tenant in the country. The "Young Ireland" revolt of 1848 swiftly fizzled out, and the Fenian rebellion of 1867 had no greater success.

The Fenians (another name for the IRB) nevertheless kept the flame of rebellion alive for the next thirty years. This secret society was especially strong in America, and was linked with the *Clan na Gael*, an open Irish-American organization that supplied aid and sympathy to the Irish nationalists. The United States, with its large Irish community (especially in Boston), acted as a kind of reservoir for militant Irish nationalism throughout the period between the Fenian rebellion and the Easter Rising.

Myth, Poetry, and
Hurley Sticks

It is always difficult to judge what effect culture has on politics. Is man's behavior influenced by poetry or propaganda? Are battles won by guns or newspapers? Years after the Easter Rising, the poet W. B. Yeats, thinking of his play about Ireland, *Cathleen ni Houlihan*, was to ask himself:

> Did that play of mine send out
> Certain men the English shot?

What is certain is that the remarkable Irish "renaissance" of the later nineteenth century encouraged, sometimes very directly, the growth of nationalist feeling in Ireland.

In 1884 a man named Michael Cusack (he appears as "the Citizen" in James Joyce's novel *Ulysses*) founded the Gaelic Athletic Association (GAA) to encourage the playing of native Irish games, such as hurling, rather than the English sports that were officially encouraged. A sports association may not seem dangerously subversive, but the GAA took its aims very seriously. Its members were not only encouraged to take part in Irish games, they were flatly forbidden to play English ones. The association revived local patriotism through competitions, and local patriotism could easily be turned into national patriotism. Significantly, Michael Cusack was closely associated with members of the IRB.

A more intellectual stimulus to nationalism was provided by the Gaelic League, founded in 1893 by, among others, Eoin Mac-Neill, a professor of early Irish history. The Gaelic League was the most important of a number of scholarly societies founded about this time to promote the study of the Irish language and literature. Many of the people involved were members of the Anglo-Irish "Ascendancy." Some were Protestants, some even had titles (like Lady Gregory, who established the famous Abbey Theater in Dublin), and some of those who enthusiastically encouraged Irish literature could not speak Irish themselves. Yeats was one of these.

The Gaelic League was supposed to be nonpolitical, but a position of neutrality became increasingly difficult to uphold. Dublin literary society was torn between those who were primarily interested in art, and those who believed that art must serve a political purpose and furiously attacked J. M. Synge's *In the Shadow of the Glen* (1903) because it portrayed an Irish woman who was unfaithful to her husband ("all of us know," said Arthur Griffith, "that Irish women are the most virtuous in the world"). Four years later, Synge's most famous play, *The Playboy of the Western World*, provoked a riot and its performance was stopped.

Besides these extraordinary developments in literature, the Dublin press turned out a large number of lively newspapers, advocating a variety of policies, including treason (which, however, usually led to the suppression of the paper concerned). One of the most remarkable was *The Leader*, edited by a tough journalist named D. P. Moran, which opposed not only Britain and all its works but also the Irish parliamentary party — pale copies of Englishmen, according to Moran — and the Anglo-Irish literary movement. Indeed, it was sometimes hard to see what, if anything, Moran actually approved of.

Sinn Fein

The most influential of all the nationalist newspapers in Ireland was the *United Irishman*, first issued in 1899 under the editorship of Arthur Griffith, then aged twenty-eight. Griffith was a militant nationalist, who, while ruling out armed rebellion as impractical, wanted to end Ireland's dependence on England in every area of public life. A brilliantly savage journalist, he characterized "John Bull" (the British version of Uncle Sam) as a brigand with one hand on Ireland's throat and the other in her pocket.

Griffith was not long content with negative criticism. In the early 1900's he formed a new nationalist organization, which acquired the name *Sinn Fein* ("Ourselves"). The crux of Sinn Fein policy was a boycott of all things British. Elected Irish representatives should refuse to attend the British Parliament in London and should deny its right to authority in Ireland. Instead they should form an Irish Parliament, in Ireland. Young Irishmen should not enlist in the British army. The two countries should be separated completely, except for the monarch, who should reign as king of England and of Ireland. Griffith's model was the dual monarchy of Austria and Hungary, which the Hungarians had forced upon Austria by roughly the same methods as Griffith advocated in Ireland. In the economic field, Ireland should set up a tariff barrier to promote the growth of Irish industries and end dependence on British manufactures.

The Sinn Fein movement gathered strength quite rapidly for a year or two, but it failed to win mass support. Although there were over one hundred Sinn Fein societies in 1908, they were all very small, and Griffith's newspaper (renamed *Sinn Fein*) was constantly on the verge of bankruptcy. In the same year, Sinn

Arthur Griffith.

Fein put up a candidate to run against the representative of Redmond's Irish parliamentary party at a by-election (a by-election is an election for a single district, as distinct from a general election for the whole country). The Sinn Fein candidate was easily beaten, gaining only a quarter of the votes cast. After this setback, Sinn Fein kept clear of elections, and it began to look as though this promising organization would gently fade away like so many others.

The Labor Movement

By comparison with most Western countries at the end of the nineteenth century, Ireland had an extremely small class of industrial workers, and labor organization was weak. Trade unions flourish best when there is a high demand for labor, but in underdeveloped Ireland there were few skilled jobs available, and there was always a plentiful supply of unskilled labor, despite emigration, from among dispossessed and unemployed farmers. Moreover, the Irish trade unions were usually dominated by parent unions in England.

The placid industrial scene was shattered during the early 1900's largely through the efforts of James Larkin and James Connolly.

Although Connolly appeared on the scene first, it was Larkin who made the biggest headlines between 1907 and 1914. A great bull of a man who needed no microphones to carry his voice to an open-air meeting of thousands, Larkin was moved by simple feelings: sympathy for the poor and hatred for the employers who exploited them. He had terrific courage and self-confidence, and he cared for no individual, however exalted, nor for any institution, however venerable. Roaring threats and defiance, he blasted tyrannical bosses and servile trade unionists alike.

His work began in Belfast, where he organized dockers and other low-paid workers and managed, although temporarily, to unite Protestant and Catholic workers against their bosses. Some trades gained higher wages, but the dock strike that Larkin organized ended in failure. The employers were simply too powerful and the workers too weak.

If conditions were bad in Belfast, they were worse in Dublin.

Even Larkin was shocked by the dreadful state of the Dublin slums. Over two thousand families (about six thousand people) lived in single rooms with no heat or light or lavatories. Disease was widespread: according to one historian, the death rate in Dublin was higher than in Calcutta, a city notorious for ghastly living conditions. Wages in Dublin were extremely low; skilled jobs were few, and unemployment was nearly 20 percent. In the slums, any spare pennies were usually spent on liquor, while many women resorted to prostitution to buy food.

Larkin set to work organizing the dockers, the porters, and the general laborers and, having quarreled with the British headquarters of the existing unions, established the Irish Transport and General Workers' Union (ITGWU) in 1909. He attracted many workers away from the old unions and secured some rises in wages. All this was accomplished amid turmoil, strikes, and violence. Larkin himself was imprisoned for several weeks.

In 1910 Larkin's movement was vigorously reinforced by the return from America (where he had spent the previous seven years) of James Connolly.

Connolly was to become one of the leaders — perhaps the most impressive of the leaders — of the Easter Rising of 1916. He was a truly remarkable man, and his death before a British firing squad was surely a disaster for Ireland. He was born in Ireland in 1868 but was raised in Edinburgh, Scotland, for his parents, like so many others, had been forced by economic hardship to leave Ireland. Although he never had an education worthy of the name, Connolly was an intellectual, with a wide knowledge of history and a profound grasp of the doctrines of socialism. Although he was not an orthodox Marxist, his aims in 1916 were both independence from Britain and political revolution within

Ireland itself. This set him apart from the other leaders of the Rising, most of whom were relatively ignorant of political ideology. Historians have discussed at length whether Connolly was a nationalist first and a socialist second or the other way around. But for Connolly the two creeds could not be separated.

As a result of his socialist activities, he had to leave Edinburgh in 1896. He went to Dublin to work for the Dublin Socialist Society and for a time managed to support his wife and children on the laughable wage of one pound (then about five dollars) a week. For seven years he struggled to convert the apathetic Irish masses to his belief in a free, socialist state. He wrote,

> The struggle for Irish freedom has two aspects: it is national and it is social. The national ideal can never be realised until Ireland stands forth before the world as a nation, free and independent. It is social and economic because no matter what the form of government may be, as long as one class owns as private property the land and instruments of labour from which mankind derive their substance, that class will always have it in their power to plunder and enslave the remainder of their fellow creatures.

Thus Connolly realized that the root of the Irish question was economic (the ownership by one class of "the land and instruments of labour"), but the first step to a solution would have to be political (a free Ireland).

In the end, the socialist movement was to be swallowed up by the nationalist movement, but had Connolly lived, the outcome might have been different.

James Connolly.

In 1903 Connolly left for America, where he could better provide for his family. When he returned in 1910, he became an organizer for Larkin's union in Ulster and was soon recognized as a labor leader second only to Larkin.

The years 1911–13 witnessed widespread industrial unrest, in Britain as well as in Ireland. The membership of Larkin's union doubled in a single year, and he succeeded in gaining wage increases and other benefits for the transport workers. In 1913 he clashed with the Dublin Employers' Federation, who decided to smash his union by means of a lock-out. (A lock-out is like a strike in reverse: the employers lock the doors against their workers, refusing to allow them to work.) As a result of strikes and lock-outs, some 25,000 men were out of work in Dublin in the fall of 1913. Larkin was arrested as he began to address a crowd, a riot broke out, and two people were killed when the Dublin police reacted with undue violence.

Connolly had also been arrested, but the hard-pressed workers, with help from British trade unions, still refused to surrender. Unfortunately Larkin, when he was released from jail, antagonized the British unions by his violent language, and their contributions stopped. The Dublin strikers were gradually forced back to work on the employers' terms. Although Larkin's union was not destroyed, it had suffered a disastrous defeat. Larkin sailed for America in 1914 and did not return until 1923. His departure left Connolly preeminent among militant labor leaders.

In 1913 a former army officer had suggested to Larkin and Connolly that military drill might improve the morale of the un-

Members of the Irish Citizen Army parade outside their headquarters, Liberty Hall.

26

employed men. Both leaders agreed, and the Irish Citizen Army was founded. This was one of the two military bodies that would take part in the Easter Rising. Its members vowed to sink all differences of birth and religion in the common cause of the Irish nation and public ownership. The Citizen Army was extremely small — it never had many more than 300 members — but, as the right arm of James Connolly, it was to prove very much more powerful than its numbers suggested.

The Irish Volunteers

It would hardly be possible to list all the nationalist societies of one kind or another that appeared in Ireland during the twenty years before the Easter Rising. Most of them were tiny and their aims varied widely (only a few openly supported revolutionary tactics), while the same people could often be found running several different organizations.

One man whose nationalist activities were particularly numerous was Bulmer Hobson, like many nationalist leaders an Ulsterman, and the son of middle-class Quaker parents. An excellent organizer, he had been a member of the Gaelic League and the Gaelic Athletic Association. He was one of the most energetic members of the IRB and a leading contributor to its newspaper, *Irish Freedom.* With the enthusiastic support of Countess Markievicz, an Irishwoman who had married a Polish count, he also organized a youth movement called the *Fianna.* He established this organization in Belfast to encourage an interest in Irish sports and the Irish language among Irish boys, but the national movement was primarily political. The boys swore to "work for the independence of Ireland," and the Fianna became a kind of nursery for the IRB.

The IRB had gone into a decline after the Fenian rebellion of 1867, but in the early 1900's, benefiting from the general revival of nationalism, it perked up. The old leaders had mostly faded out, and more dynamic, younger men came to the top. Most famous of them was Sean MacDermott (or Mac Diarmada, as he later called himself), who graduated to the IRB from Sinn Fein. For eight years he was its national organizer, riding about the country on a bicycle and gaining recruits for the revolutionary

Tom Clarke.

organization from the ranks of the Gaelic Athletic Association and the Gaelic League. It was the charming but ruthless MacDermott who was largely responsible for replacing the nonpolitical chairman of the Gaelic League with a dedicated revolutionary, Patrick H. Pearse.

MacDermott himself had been recruited into the IRB by Thomas J. Clarke, a mild and dusty-looking little man who ran a tobacconist's shop in Dublin. Tom Clarke was, in fact, the last remaining representative of the old Fenians among the leaders of the 1916 Rising. Despite his harmless appearance, he was utterly dedicated to the destruction of British power, and it is hard to imagine him in any role other than that of the uncompromising revolutionary. He had spent fifteen years in a particularly tough British prison, but his spirit was unbroken.

The introduction of the third home rule bill in the British Parliament had set off a fierce Unionist reaction. In Ulster thousands of people had signed (some of them in their own blood) the "Solemn League and Covenant," swearing "to defeat the present conspiracy to set up a Home Rule Parliament in Ireland," and Sir Edward Carson had presided over the formation of the Ulster Volunteers, an unofficial army dedicated to the preservation of the union.

The southern Irish were quick to follow Ulster's example, and the Irish Volunteers were formed soon afterward, in November 1913. The prime mover in this case was Eoin MacNeill, who has already been mentioned as a founder of the Gaelic League.

Of all the events leading up to the Easter Rising, the creation of the Volunteers under MacNeill was perhaps the most important. The IRB could have formed its own private army, and in fact Bulmer Hobson had taken some steps toward doing so, but

the IRB did not command mass support. Moreover, as a supposedly secret society, it could hardly attempt large-scale recruiting. But MacNeill, a professor at University College, Dublin, was a well-known and widely respected man who, though a nationalist, was considered a moderate. It was generally assumed that his political views were more or less the same as those of John Redmond and the Irish parliamentary party.

The purpose of the Volunteers was described by MacNeill as "defensive and protective." The Volunteers would "not contemplate either aggression or domination." The behavior of the Unionists, in Britain as well as in Ulster, had shown that military force was likely to be a decisive factor in future relations between Britain and Ireland. It was necessary for the Irish to take measures to protect their rights — hence the Volunteers. The movement was immediately successful. Its membership reached 100,000 in little more than six months, and it continued to grow after that.

John Redmond viewed the formation of the Irish Volunteers with some apprehension. He and his party were the representatives of the great majority of Irish nationalists and from his point of view it was necessary that he should have some control over the new movement. MacNeill and his colleagues risked a disastrous split in the Volunteers if they tried to keep Redmond out, and they therefore agreed to Redmond's demand that twenty-five moderate Home Rulers should be appointed to the governing committee. For the time being, Redmond had gained apparent control of the Volunteers, and the more militant of MacNeill's associates seemed to have been outmaneuvered.

Eoin MacNeill.

Arms for Ireland

An army, even a "defensive and protective" one, is not much use without guns, and the British government's first response to the formation of the Volunteers was to prohibit the import of firearms (although no attempt was made to suppress the Volunteers). MacNeill was equally worried by the absence of funds with which to buy guns, illegal or not.

Once again, Ulster showed the way. On an April night in 1914, Carson's men landed a large consignment of guns and ammunition on the coast north of Belfast. The British authorities appeared reluctant to prevent them and this, coming soon after an incident known as the Curragh Mutiny, when a number of British army officers threatened to resign rather than fight the Ulster Unionists, confirmed the suspicion of Irish nationalists that the British authorities were biased in favor of the Ulster rebels.

The danger of civil war grew. In their efforts to obtain guns, the representatives of the Irish Volunteers were assisted by several well-to-do Anglo-Irish men and women who, though not republicans, felt that Ulster's successful gun-running operation had given them an unfair advantage. These people provided most of the money for buying weapons in Germany, and one of them, Erskine Childers, lent his yacht to carry the guns into Howth Harbor on July 26, 1914.

The operation was carried out smoothly — in broad daylight — but later in the day a party of soldiers, being jeered for their failure to prevent the delivery of the guns, fired on the crowd. Three people were killed and thirty-two wounded. The incident might well have sparked off a serious riot in Dublin, but news of the killings was overshadowed by impending world war.

34

The "Blood Sacrifice"

Upon the outbreak of World War I, John Redmond made a patriotic speech in which he announced that the Irish Volunteers would garrison Ireland, releasing British soldiers for the war in Europe. A few days later he went further, promising that the Volunteers would themselves fight for Britain against Germany.

Redmond had made a political blunder — the result of his loyalty to the British empire and his loss of touch with the people he represented. Militant nationalists, of course, had never had any time for him; Arthur Griffith regarded him and his party as a worse obstacle to Irish freedom than the British. But Redmond's impulsive promise offended a far wider range of Irish people and caused a split in the Volunteers. Although the great majority remained loyal to him, some 11,000, led by Eoin MacNeill, broke away (but kept the name "Irish Volunteers").

The governing body of the Volunteers was reorganized. While MacNeill remained the chief, several members of the new executive council (Patrick H. Pearse, Thomas MacDonagh, Joseph Plunkett, and, later, Eamonn Ceannt) were also leading members of the IRB. In fact, from the time of the break with Redmond, it seems that IRB members had infiltrated the Volunteers so thoroughly that they were in a position to take over. MacNeill never knew this, and for the time being the IRB members were lying low.

It is important to remember that there were several different kinds of nationalists in Ireland in 1914. Broadly speaking they could be divided into three main types: those like Redmond whose loyalty to the British empire came first; those like Mac-Neill, loyal only to Ireland but unwilling to use force against

Patrick Pearse.

Britain; and those like Pearse and Connolly, who remembered the old saying, "England's difficulty is Ireland's opportunity," and waited only for a suitable moment to launch a rebellion.

Patrick Henry Pearse was the outstanding representative of the IRB leaders. Like his comrades MacDonagh and Plunkett, he was a poet and was immersed in the legends and history of Ireland. So intense was his patriotism that to him "Ireland" was more than a nation, more than an idea, more than a person. He had been in the forefront of the movement to popularize Irish poetry and the Irish language, and he had founded a famous school, Saint Enda's, where Gaelic was taught and spoken. There, the boys were taught to revere the ancient Irish hero, Cú Chulainn, whose words, painted on the wall, confronted the visitor to Saint Enda's: "I care not though I were to live but one day and one night, if only my fame and my deeds live after me." Pearse's dedicated idealism, together with his passionate oratory, was to make him, with Connolly, chief among the leaders of the Easter Rising.

Pearse did not expect to survive the rebellion, but he hoped, by a dramatic act, to waken Ireland from her apathy. He did not really think about overthrowing the British or establishing the republic. The Rising would be a "blood sacrifice." A devout Catholic, Pearse did not hesitate to compare it with another, greater sacrifice — Christ crucified. Pearse and those who shared his feelings went out consciously into the Dublin streets:

> To break themselves and die, they and a few,
> In bloody protest for a glorious thing.

A glorious thing. Whatever doubts we may have about the motives of martyrs, whatever one's sympathies with the Irish nationalists, it is impossible to remain unmoved by the intense self-sacrifice of Patrick Pearse and his friends. Yeats, a greater poet than Pearse, was later to catch the emotion in lines that have become famous:

> We know their dream; enough
> To know they dreamed and are dead;
> And what if excess of love
> Bewildered them 'till they died?
> I write it out in a verse —
> MacDonagh and MacBride
> And Connolly and Pearse
> Now and in time to be,
> Wherever green is worn,
> Are changed, changed utterly:
> A terrible beauty is born.

Pearse and Connolly

Within the inner circles of the IRB, plans for an insurrection began to be discussed as soon as the European war started in August 1914. In New York, representatives of *Clan na Gael* met the German ambassador to ask for military aid. In Dublin, the IRB leaders decided on a rebellion with or without German help. Secrecy was of the utmost importance, for it would have been fatal to the plan if either the British or the official leadership of the Volunteers had learned what was afoot.

To mount a serious rebellion, it was necessary to have a reasonably large, armed force of men, and that could only be provided by the Volunteers (Connolly's Citizen Army numbered about three hundred). MacNeill, however, would not approve a rising. He ruled that the Volunteers' function was defensive and they should fight only if they were attacked or if the authorities tried to suppress them.

The activities of Connolly and his Citizen Army also posed a threat to IRB plans. Connolly was not a member of the IRB and knew nothing of their activities. Throughout 1915 he became increasingly restless at the lack of action, and there was a serious danger that he would forestall the IRB by leading the Citizen Army in a rising of his own.

None of the militant nationalists shared Connolly's socialist ideas; in fact, they had given surprisingly little thought to what kind of society they would create after the British had been thrown out. But to some extent Pearse was an exception. He had written that "no private right to property is good as against the public right of the nation," which is a fair starting point for a socialist state. Although the two men were of strikingly different types, it

39

was probably Pearse who was chiefly responsible for the dramatic coalition of the Irish Citizen Army and the Irish Volunteers in January 1916. The alliance was formed during the course of three mysterious days, when Connolly suddenly vanished, reappearing without explanation on the third day. He had been in secret conference with the military council of the IRB, who told him of their plans — the date of the Rising had already been fixed — and asked him to join them. From that time onward, Connolly cooperated fully with Pearse and the other leaders of the Rising.

Nevertheless, Connolly remained on his guard. He kept half an eye on the future — on what would happen after the Rising. A week before it was due to begin, he told the Citizen Army: "The odds are a thousand to one against us. If we win, we'll be great heroes; but if we lose we'll be the greatest scoundrels the country ever produced. In the event of victory, hold on to your rifles, as those with whom we are fighting may stop before our goal is reached. We are out for economic as well as political liberty." It has been suggested that by "those with whom we are fighting" Connolly meant MacNeill and the moderates among the Volunteers, but it seems more likely that he was thinking of Pearse, Clarke, MacDermott, and company as well.

Sir Roger Casement

Despite the successful gun-running at Howth in 1914, the Volunteers were still short of weapons. One of the men who had been engaged in the Howth operation, Sir Roger Casement, tried to wring more military assistance from Germany.

Sir Roger Casement is the Don Quixote of Irish nationalism. Handsome, intelligent, and humane — altogether an attractive character — he seemed to lose touch with reality, and his mission was an utter failure.

An Anglo-Irish Protestant, Casement had served with distinction in the British foreign service. He had been responsible for publicizing the vicious exploitation of African labor by European bosses in the Congo and elsewhere, and he had earned a knighthood before retiring in 1912. At that time he was not yet fifty years old and was already becoming deeply concerned with the affairs of Ireland.

After the Rising, the British, afraid of making Casement a martyr, tried to blacken his reputation by publishing his so-called "Black Diaries," which revealed him to be a homosexual. Many people believed (and still believe) that the diaries were a forgery.

Casement had always said that a war between Britain and Germany, which he realized was inevitable, would be "Ireland's opportunity." When the war did break out, he took on the job of secret ambassador to Germany. He happened to be in New York at the time, so it was not difficult for him to reach Germany (the United States was then a neutral). He wanted three things from the Germans: support for an Irish declaration of independence, a supply of arms, and a brigade of men, whom he hoped to recruit from Irish prisoners of war in German camps. Although the Germans did eventually send some arms, that was not the result of Casement's mission, and his other aims remained unfulfilled.

Nor were Casement's activities as well disguised as he hoped. Britain's brilliant department of naval intelligence (the famous "Room 40") had cracked the German codes, and messages passing between Germany and America were simultaneously decoded in London. Casement's movements were being tracked.

Eventually Casement became disillusioned with the Germans, who told him flatly that they would do nothing to help Ireland unless they were sure it would also benefit Germany. He believed that even the promised rifles would not be sent, and he therefore returned to Ireland hoping to prevent the rebellion which, without German assistance, he knew was hopeless. On the eve of the Rising he landed on the southwest coast from a German U-boat. He was nearly drowned coming ashore, and, within a few hours of landing, was arrested by the police as a suspicious character.

The *Aud* Sinks

Despite Casement's fears, the Germans did send arms. A German ship, masquerading as a Norwegian tanker under the name *Aud*, sailed from Lübeck on April 9 (three days before Casement departed in the U-boat). She carried twenty thousand rifles, which the Germans had captured from the Russians, as well as ten machine guns and one million rounds of ammunition.

The plan was for the *Aud* to rendezvous with Casement and for the arms to be handed over to Irish Volunteers at Tralee Bay on April 20 (the Thursday before Easter). For some extraordinary reason, the *Aud* carried no radio, and as a result of late changes in plan, neither the U-boat nor — more important — the Volunteers were at the rendezvous.

The *Aud*'s captain, Karl Spindler, hung about in the bay for a time and successfully bluffed an armed British trawler that came alongside to investigate. By midday on Friday, he had realized that something had gone wrong, and he decided to wait no longer in British waters. But soon after leaving the bay, the *Aud* was intercepted, and this time the British insisted that she put into Queenstown Harbor for inspection. Captain Spindler gave the order to scuttle the ship rather than let the British capture her cargo. Early on Saturday morning, just outside Queenstown Harbor, the *Aud* went to the bottom. Down with her went the twenty thousand rifles and the ten invaluable machine guns, and down too went the last chance that the Easter Rising might succeed.

The Rising Postponed

Immediately before the Rising, events moved very swiftly, and as the most vital developments were still cloaked in secrecy, the story is a complicated one. The effectiveness of IRB security is well illustrated by the fact that on April 19, four days before the date set for the Rising to begin, Eoin MacNeill, head of the Irish Volunteers, still knew nothing about it.

Although he was opposed to the idea of an insurrection, MacNeill had conceded that the Volunteers should defend themselves if the British authorities made any move toward suppressing or disarming them. The "Castle document," which was shown to the Volunteers' executive on April 17, seemed to suggest that the moment had arrived. The "Castle document" was said to be a government order for the suppression of the Volunteers. It was almost certainly a forgery (some historians have seen in it the crafty hand of Sean MacDermott), but MacNeill was convinced. He sent out a general order to the Volunteers warning them to prepare to resist by force. Thus the aims of the militants were achieved: the Volunteers were mobilized.

However, things soon started to go wrong. On the night of April 19, Bulmer Hobson, who was an associate of MacNeill's, learned that some divisional leaders of the Volunteers had already received orders to prepare for a full-scale rising against the British. He immediately took this news to MacNeill.

MacNeill realized that he had been double-crossed by the militants and drove to the house where Pearse lived with his mother. Angry words were exchanged, and Pearse frankly ad-

Asquith — British prime minister at the time of the Rising.

mitted that the IRB had all along been planning to use the Volunteers for a purpose that MacNeill would never have countenanced. MacNeill left the house, threatening that he would do everything he could to prevent the Rising, short of telephoning the British authorities.

The next day (Good Friday) MacNeill met again with Pearse and with MacDermott and MacDonagh — and he changed his mind. He was told that it was too late to stop the Rising and he also learned for the first time of the arms expected from Germany (the *Aud* had been intercepted several hours earlier, but the news had not reached Dublin). The militants breathed again, but to prevent further hitches they "kidnapped" Bulmer Hobson and kept him out of the way for a day.

MacNeill had been placed in an impossible position, and he can hardly be blamed for his pendulum swings for and against the Rising during these frantic hours. On Saturday, he heard that the *Aud*'s cargo had been lost, and at the same time a Volunteer officer named Sean Fitzgibbon showed him evidence that suggested that the "Castle document" was a forgery. He went to Saint Enda's school, where he had another angry interview with Pearse. The Rising was not set to begin until Sunday evening; MacNeill just had time to send countermanding orders to most of the Volunteers' detachments and to insert in the *Sunday Independent* a notice that announced: "All orders for special action are hereby cancelled . . ." Everyone knew, or could guess, what "special action" meant, and the British authorities, who had at last become convinced that a major insurrection was planned, relaxed their guard when they read MacNeill's announcement.

Pearse, Connolly, and the other leaders held a meeting on Sunday morning in Liberty Hall (headquarters of the Irish Cit-

Liberty Hall after the Rising.

izen Army). Afterward they sent a message to MacNeill saying that all "parades" had been stopped in accordance with his instructions. What they did not say was that the orders sent out to divisional leaders had not *canceled* instructions for the Rising, but merely *postponed* them. The Rising was to begin at noon on the following day.

Easter Sunday ended quietly. That morning, Dubliners had stood in the churches and sung "Christ is risen!" The next day, they would be whispering behind their doors "Ireland is risen!"

Dublin Castle

On April 10, less than two weeks before the date set for the Rising, the chief of British intelligence in Dublin, Major Price, submitted a report on security: "The general state of Ireland, apart from recruiting and apart from the activities of the pro-German Sinn Fein minority, is thoroughly satisfactory. The mass of the people are sound and loyal as regards the war, and the country is in a very prosperous state and very free from ordinary crime."

A notably misleading estimate! Yet British intelligence was by no means as incapable as this report suggests, and Major Price's view that the mass of the people were sound and loyal was reasonably accurate. (It is important to remember that for each Irishman who fought against Britain during the Easter Rising, there were a hundred Irishmen fighting for Britain against Germany.)

Why did the Easter Rising catch the British unawares? Part of the trouble was the character of the British administration in Ireland. At its head was the lord lieutenant, an office that had become one of prestige rather than power, although Lord Wimborne, who was lord lieutenant in 1916, was more active in the administration than were his predecessors. The real head of the executive was the chief secretary. Augustine Birrell had been appointed to that post in 1907 and he was still there in 1916 — an unusually long tenure.

As chief secretary for Ireland, Birrell was a British cabinet minister (at one time he had been mentioned as a possible future prime minister). His seat in the cabinet gave him more power, but it also meant that he had to divide his time between Dublin and London. Birrell did not really enjoy crossing the Irish Sea, and by

Dublin Castle — headquarters of the British authorities.

1916 his visits to Dublin had become infrequent. During his absence, the undersecretary held the fort — or rather, the castle, for Dublin Castle was the headquarters of the British administration.

Augustine Birrell was an amiable, witty, book-loving man who, at the age of sixty-six (in 1916), was unlikely to obtain a higher political office. Nor did he show any ambition to do so (his critics suggested that he was rather lazy). As a lifelong Liberal, he was in sympathy with John Redmond and the Home Rule party and, an agnostic himself, he was more sympathetic to Irish Catholics than to Ulster Protestants. As he said at the time of the Ulster crisis in 1913, when it seemed that Ireland was about to split in two: "I would sooner be split by the Babylonian whore [the Church of Rome] than by Sir Edward Carson."

In April 1916, Birrell was in London, though he was in almost daily contact with Sir Matthew Nathan, the undersecretary, in Dublin Castle. A distinguished civil servant, Sir Matthew had been appointed in October 1914. Thus he had been in Ireland for only eighteen months at the time of the Rising. (The lord lieutenant, Lord Wimborne, had an even shorter experience with Irish affairs, having been appointed in 1915.) Nathan's political beliefs coincided fairly closely with Birrell's and, as a Jew, Nathan was not biased in favor of either Catholics or Protestants. In general, he and Birrell got along well together.

The government of Ireland, as personified by Birrell and Nathan, suffered from the handicap of all liberal governments in a potentially revolutionary situation. On the left was the Sinn Fein movement (the name Sinn Fein had come to describe the militant nationalist movement as a whole, although the Sinn Fein party organization led by Arthur Griffith did not take part in the Rising). On the right were the Unionists and the police and mili-

tary authorities. Birrell was very reluctant to use repressive measures in Ireland, and he therefore tended to play down the threat from the "Sinn Feiners" and to brush off the warnings of doom that assailed him from the right. His policy was not only humane but, in general, correct: as Major Price said, most people were loyal. However, when the Rising found Dublin Castle unprepared, Birrell's policy was, naturally enough, discredited.

Dublin Castle was unprepared — but not entirely ignorant. Rumors of an intended rebellion had been circulating for months. British intelligence in London had unmasked some of the plans and had observed Sir Roger Casement's activities although, as a result of poor communications, Dublin Castle knew less than British naval intelligence about Casement's movements. Finally, the capture of the *Aud* showed beyond reasonable doubt that an armed insurrection was imminent. Lord Wimborne wanted to arrest the Sinn Fein leaders at once, and if this had been done the Rising might have been stopped. But Sir Matthew Nathan was unwilling to act without authorization from Birrell in London, and the publication of MacNeill's message canceling the maneuvers of the Volunteers suggested that there was no immediate danger. Nevertheless, it was decided to proceed with Lord Wimborne's suggestion, assuming Birrell agreed, on Tuesday. On Monday morning, therefore, Nathan was in his office in Dublin Castle discussing plans with Major Price, when they were disturbed by the sound of shots . . .

Augustine Birrell — chief secretary for Ireland.

At the G.P.O.

Shortly before midday on Easter Monday, April 24, James Connolly, commandant of the Dublin forces, led his company of men from Liberty Hall, down Abbey Street, and halted them opposite the grand classical facade of Dublin's General Post Office (G.P.O.). Some of the men wore the dark green uniform of the Citizen Army, others the lighter green of the Irish Volunteers. A greater number wore no uniform at all. Their weapons also suggested a nonprofessional army: some had rifles, some had shotguns, some had no guns at all; yet they marched and drilled with precision. They had been practicing for a long time.

"Company, halt!" Connolly, a stocky figure in green uniform and slouch hat, briefly surveyed his men. "Left turn. The G.P.O. . . . CHARGE!"

Within a few minutes, the green, orange, and white flag of the Irish Republic was fluttering from the flagpole. Patrick Pearse walked out onto the steps of the building, a single sheet of paper in his hand: "Irishmen and Irishwomen," he read to the curious crowd gathering in the street, "In the name of God and of the dead generations from which she receives her old tradition of nationhood, Ireland, through us, summons her children to her flag and strikes for her freedom. . . ." The document was signed by seven men: Thomas J. Clarke, Sean Mac Diarmada (Mac-Dermott), Thomas MacDonagh, P. H. Pearse, Eamonn Ceannt, James Connolly, and Joseph Plunkett.

The G.P.O., Dublin.

POBLACHT NA H EIREANN.

THE PROVISIONAL GOVERNMENT
OF THE
IRISH REPUBLIC
TO THE PEOPLE OF IRELAND.

IRISHMEN AND IRISHWOMEN : In the name of God and of the dead generations from which she receives her old tradition of nationhood, Ireland, through us, summons her children to her flag and strikes for her freedom.

Having organised and trained her manhood through her secret revolutionary organisation, the Irish Republican Brotherhood, and through her open military organisations, the Irish Volunteers and the Irish Citizen Army, having patiently perfected her discipline, having resolutely waited for the right moment to reveal itself, she now seizes that moment, and, supported by her exiled children in America and by gallant allies in Europe, but relying in the first on her own strength, she strikes in full confidence of victory.

We declare the right of the people of Ireland to the ownership of Ireland, and to the unfettered control of Irish destinies, to be sovereign and indefeasible. The long usurpation of that right by a foreign people and government has not extinguished the right, nor can it ever be extinguished except by the destruction of the Irish people. In every generation the Irish people have asserted their right to national freedom and sovereignty ; six times during the past three hundred years they have asserted it in arms. Standing on that fundamental right and again asserting it in arms in the face of the world, we hereby proclaim the Irish Republic as a Sovereign Independent State, and we pledge our lives and the lives of our comrades-in-arms to the cause of its freedom, of its welfare, and of its exaltation among the nations.

The Irish Republic is entitled to, and hereby claims, the allegiance of every Irishman and Irishwoman. The Republic guarantees religious and civil liberty, equal rights and equal opportunities to all its citizens, and declares its resolve to pursue the happiness and prosperity of the whole nation and of all its parts, cherishing all the children of the nation equally, and oblivious of the differences carefully fostered by an alien government, which have divided a minority from the majority in the past.

Until our arms have brought the opportune moment for the establishment of a permanent National Government, representative of the whole people of Ireland and elected by the suffrages of all her men and women, the Provisional Government, hereby constituted, will administer the civil and military affairs of the Republic in trust for the people.

We place the cause of the Irish Republic under the protection of the Most High God, Whose blessing we invoke upon our arms, and we pray that no one who serves that cause will dishonour it by cowardice, inhumanity, or rapine. In this supreme hour the Irish nation must, by its valour and discipline and by the readiness of its children to sacrifice themselves for the common good, prove itself worthy of the august destiny to which it is called.

Signed on Behalf of the Provisional Government,

THOMAS J. CLARKE,

SEAN Mac DIARMADA, THOMAS MacDONAGH,

P. H. PEARSE, EAMONN CEANNT,

JAMES CONNOLLY. JOSEPH PLUNKETT.

The crowd listened in silence; a few people laughed; others hurried away before the police arrived. But Connolly stepped up to Pearse and shook him warmly by the hand. "Thanks be to God, Pearse, that we have lived to see this day." His joy was sincere, yet this was the man who a few hours before had said to a friend, "Bill, we are going out to be slaughtered."

Proclamation of the Irish republic.

Easter Week

The Rising was intended to be a national rebellion, but as a result of MacNeill's countermanding order on Easter Sunday and bad communications in general, it was confined, except for a few isolated outbreaks elsewhere, to the city of Dublin. Even there, the confusion of orders and the last-minute postponement resulted in a very poor turnout. Not many more than a thousand Volunteers were present on Easter Monday (a few more joined in the next few days) although nearly ten times that number should have been available. Together with about two hundred men of the Citizen Army, the total number that took part in the Rising probably never exceeded sixteen hundred. The British authorities could call on vastly superior forces equipped with sophisticated weapons, including grenades and artillery. However, these forces were scattered and unready. The Rising had the advantage of surprise; but surprise was not enough.

The plan was to seize a number of key buildings throughout the city and therefore to command the main routes along which British reinforcements would arrive. But because of the small number of men available, the plan could not be carried out very effectively, and it soon proved almost impossible to maintain communications between the key positions.

A number of avoidable mistakes were also made. At Dublin Castle, the initial attack, which had made Sir Matthew Nathan and Major Price leap to their feet in consternation, was not pressed home. There were few soldiers inside the castle on Easter Monday, a holiday, and it could probably have been captured easily. However, it was a large and rambling building and could

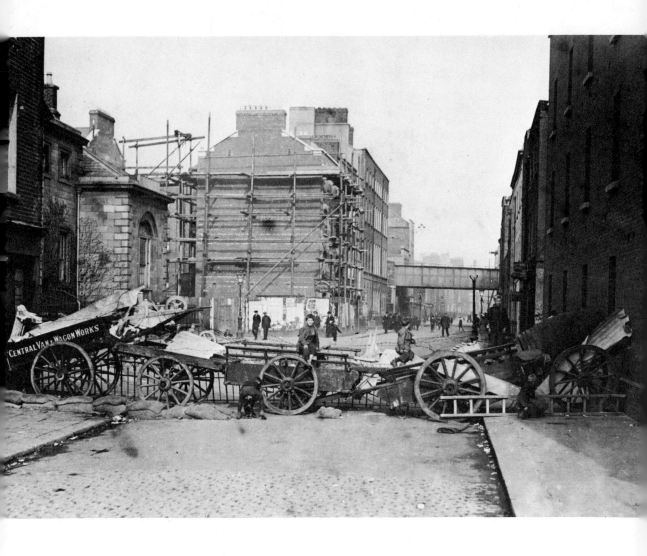

Above: Barricades were hastily erected with carts, torn-up railings, and furniture, laced together with barbed wire. Over: Street map of central Dublin.

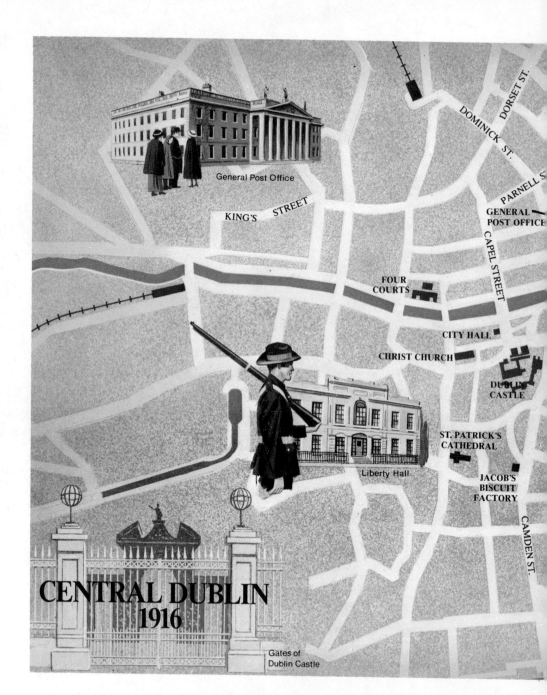

General Post Office

KING'S STREET

DORSET ST.

DOMINICK ST.

PARNELL ST.

GENERAL POST OFFICE

CAPEL STREET

FOUR COURTS

CITY HALL

CHRIST CHURCH

DUBLIN CASTLE

ST. PATRICK'S CATHEDRAL

Liberty Hall

JACOB'S BISCUIT FACTORY

CAMDEN ST.

CENTRAL DUBLIN
1916

Gates of Dublin Castle

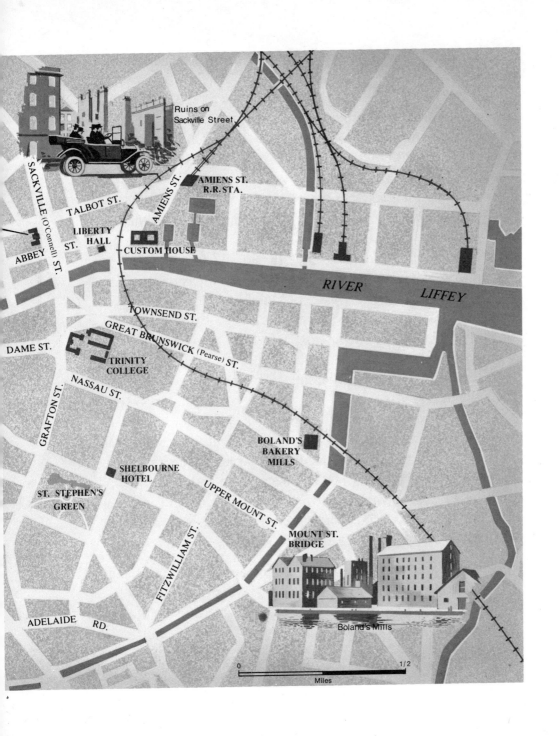

Ruins on
Sackville Street

AMIENS ST.
R.R. STA.

AMIENS ST.

TALBOT ST.

LIBERTY
HALL

SACKVILLE (O'Connell) ST.

ABBEY ST.

CUSTOM HOUSE

RIVER   LIFFEY

TOWNSEND ST.

DAME ST.

GREAT BRUNSWICK (Pearse) ST.

TRINITY
COLLEGE

NASSAU ST.

GRAFTON ST.

BOLAND'S
BAKERY
MILLS

SHELBOURNE
HOTEL

ST. STEPHEN'S
GREEN

UPPER MOUNT ST.

FITZWILLIAM ST.

MOUNT ST.
BRIDGE

Boland's Mills

ADELAIDE   RD.

0   1/2

Miles

not, perhaps, have been defended for long against a determined counterattack.

At Saint Stephen's Green, where Michael Mallin of the Citizen Army was in command with Countess Markievicz as his chief lieutenant, a tactical error was made by digging trenches in the green without first capturing the Shelbourne Hotel, a large building from which British snipers were later able to command the entire area.

There is not space in this book to recount all the incidents, heroic and horrible, that Dublin witnessed during Easter week, 1916. There were atrocities on both sides. Constable James O'Brien of the Dublin Metropolitan Police, first casualty of the Rising, was shot dead at the gates of Dublin Castle as he tried to prevent the insurgents from entering the castle yard; he was unarmed. Francis Sheehy-Skeffington, a pacifist and a much-loved man, was taken prisoner while trying to prevent looting and was shot in cold blood by a British officer who was later judged to be criminally insane.

There must have been many incidents like that witnessed by James Stephens, the Irish poet and novelist, at Saint Stephen's Green. A man went up to a hastily erected barricade and tried to retrieve his hand-cart, which had been commandeered to help build the barrier. A voice from behind a fence ordered him to leave it alone, and warning shots were fired. The man dropped the shafts and boldly walked toward the fence.

He walked slowly, bent a little forward, with one hand raised and one finger up as though he were going to make a speech. Ten guns were pointing at him, and a voice repeated many times:

British soldiers firing from behind improvised fortifications.

"Go and put back that lorry or you are a dead man. Go before I count four. One, two, three, four — "

A rifle spat at him, and in two undulating movements the man sank on himself and sagged to the ground. . . . As the poor man was being carried in, a woman plumped to her knees in the road and began not to scream but to screech. At that moment the Volunteers were hated. The men by whom I was and who were lifting the body, roared into the railings:

"We'll be coming back for you, damn you."

From the railings there came no reply, and in an instant the place was again desert and silent, and the little green vistas were slumbering among the trees.

There were also moments of humor. Desmond Fitzgerald, in charge of stores at the G.P.O., was accosted by a man who noisily informed him, "I want a bottle of stout [beer]. I'm one of Jim Larkin's men. Is there no stout for one of Jim Larkin's men?" Fitzgerald told him that there was no stout at all, not even for one of Jim Larkin's men, but,

he only shouted the more. Finally he raised his voice and announced to the world at large "I want a drink." I then quite maliciously asked him why he had not said that before and called a girl to bring him a glass of water. At that he nearly burst. He wanted no water, he wanted stout. I told him that he could come in and see for himself that there was no stout there, and that then he would have to get out or we should have him removed by force. At that he departed gurgling with discontent.

64

Fitzgerald wrote: "Now that the Rising was a reality it was the amusing side of every incident that impressed my mind. It was only when I had time to think, or was speaking with O'Rahilly or Pearse or Joe Plunkett that the overshadowing tragedy became real."

And soon there was no time for talk. The snap of rifles was joined by the deadly rattle of machine guns, and in the beautiful spring sunshine the pleasant streets became alleys of death. Glass panes shattered suddenly, doors splintered, and artillery added its fearful bass to the rising chorus of destruction. Young men died, and old men trembled.

Pearse Surrenders

The insurgents were outnumbered from the beginning, and by Wednesday, as British reinforcements poured in, the odds were over twenty to one. At Mount Street Bridge, twelve Volunteers succeeded in keeping several companies of British infantry at bay for a whole day, but in the end they were overwhelmed. The barricades set up in the streets were smashed to bits by artillery, and the armed steamer *Helga* sailed up the Liffey River to blast Liberty Hall into an empty shell. Connolly had said that the capitalist authorities would never destroy private property. He was wrong. Large parts of Dublin were reduced to flames and rubble. Sackville Street (now O'Connell Street), a splendid eighteenth-century street lined by grand buildings, was completely wrecked for several blocks.

By Friday, the G.P.O., under a heavy barrage, had become a smoking, burning hell. Inside, Connolly lay on a stretcher, his ankle shattered by a stray bullet. Joseph Plunkett, who had been largely responsible for planning strategy in Dublin, was already dying of glandular fever and could hardly stand. Even Sean MacDermott, limping with arthritis, had stopped cracking jokes. The O'Rahilly (Michael Joseph O'Rahilly), an associate of MacNeill's who had courageously joined the rebels despite his disapproval of their plans, was shot dead leading a forlorn charge against British defense works. No one had had a good night's sleep since Sunday, if then.

The G.P.O. had to be evacuated, and the next day Pearse decided to surrender, "to prevent further slaughter." The other

Above: Remains of one of Sackville Street's grand buildings. Below: Smoke rising from the ruins in Earl Street.

*The facade of the Imperial Hotel appears undamaged, but behind
it hardly a brick remains.*

leaders agreed, believing that they had "redeemed Dublin from many shames and made her name splendid among the names of cities."

In some places, the insurgents had held out for a long time. Jacob's cookie factory still commanded the southern approach to the city center. At Boland's Mills, Commandant Eamonn de Valera (later president of Ireland) would not give up until the surrender order had been countersigned by his superior officer, Thomas MacDonagh. Before he and his men were marched away under guard, he gave his Browning automatic to a young English officer, to be handed on to De Valera's young son. Smartly in step, the prisoners moved off, and the people of Dublin watched, some with hostility in their eyes, most with indifference, a few with despair.

Total Irish casualties in the fighting (including a handful outside Dublin) were about 460 killed and 2,600 wounded.

The Firing Squads

Toward the end of Easter week, Major-General Sir John Maxwell was sent from England to take over supreme command in Ireland. Under martial law, which had been declared when the Rising began, General Maxwell's powers were unlimited. During the Rising there had been alarming rumors of a German invasion, and although the danger of German participation had been, as things turned out, vastly exaggerated, the British had received a terrible fright. It soon became evident that General Maxwell intended to prevent any possibility of a renewed outbreak by rigorous methods.

About 3,500 people were arrested. More than half of them were sent to jails in England, although most were released after further investigations. At hastily summoned courts-martial 171 people (including Countess Markievicz, the only woman among them) were tried, and all except one were convicted. The trials were held in secret, and about half of those convicted received death sentences, although only fifteen were eventually executed.

Patrick Pearse, president of the provisional government and commander-in-chief of the insurrectionary forces, was shot on May 3. With him died Thomas MacDonagh and old Tom Clarke. Next day Joseph Plunkett, having married his fiancée in his prison cell a few hours earlier, died along with three others. On May 5 Major John MacBride, who had fought against the British in the Boer War fifteen years before, was executed. On May 8 Eamonn Ceannt, Michael Mallin, and two others died. The last executions were carried out on May 12: Sean MacDermott and James Connolly, who could not stand because of his wounds and was shot sitting in a chair.

70

Sir John Maxwell, the British general sent to take command in Ireland after the outbreak of the Rising.

By that time, revulsion had set in. George Bernard Shaw, the Irish playwright, was among the first to speak out. He could not, he said, "regard as a traitor any Irishman taken in a fight for Irish independence against the British Government, which was a fair fight in everything except the enormous odds my countrymen had to face." When news of the first executions was greeted with approval in the British House of Commons, one white-faced Irish member screamed "Murder!" at the government ministers. Later, John Dillon, Redmond's best-known colleague, passionately denounced "this bloody course of executions." The *Manchester Guardian*, an influential Liberal newspaper, called the executions "an atrocity." The prime minister, Herbert Henry Asquith, moved to prevent further death sentences being carried out. Among those reprieved at almost the last moment were Countess Markievicz (because of her sex) and Eamonn de Valera.

The Rising had been a total failure: the military forces had been crushed in less than a week, the provisional government had not gained international recognition and, worst of all, the mass of the people had not been inspired to turn against their masters. Yet the defeat of the Rising, as Pearse had forecast, gained more than victory could have done. Within a few weeks, public feeling in Dublin swung dramatically to the side of the defeated nationalists. The families of imprisoned rebels were escorted on their way to church by enthusiastic crowds of well-wishers. In the words of historian Dr. R. Dudley Edwards, "the greatest achievement of the 1916 Rising was the change it brought about in the attitude of public opinion." The very date, "1916," gained an

After the inferno — British soldiers inspect the burned-out interior of the G.P.O.

*Heavy fighting took place at the Four Courts. Fire has melted
some of the tram-wire supports.*

almost magical significance, like "1776" in the United States, or "1917" in Soviet Russia.

The Rising also destroyed the grounds on which opponents of home rule, including the Conservative or Unionist party, had stood. Unionists had always maintained that Irish nationalism was a minor and insignificant force: Ireland's problems, they said, could all be cured by enlightened policies of moderate reform. The Rising demonstrated that Irish nationalism could not be discounted. Moderate reform would not do.

The Victory of Sinn Fein

Although its immediate effect seemed small, the Rising signaled a dramatic and irrevocable political change in Ireland. Briefly, what happened was that home rule — for a hundred years the goal of most Irish nationalists — was shown to be obsolete, and the Irish parliamentary party was annihilated almost at a stroke. Thus the Rising has come to appear as the decisive event of recent Irish history — a dividing line and a watershed, from which the history of the present Irish republic flows. But the Rising was also the beginning of seven terrible years of conflict, the years of "the troubles," and not all the events of those years were directly linked with the Rising, even though the fact of the Rising affected everything that happened later.

It could be argued that the destruction of Redmond's Home Rule party and the victory of Sinn Fein under Eamonn de Valera and Arthur Griffith were accomplished more by the clumsy conduct of the British authorities than by the impact of the Rising.

In the first place, reconciliation was hardly possible as long as General Maxwell remained in Ireland. But although a new chief secretary was appointed to succeed Birrell (who vanished into retirement feeling that fate had treated him unjustly), Maxwell was not recalled until November 1916, and until that time he was effectively in command in Ireland. Resentment against the British was fanned also by the publication of reports of atrocities by British troops during the Rising, by the execution of Sir Roger Casement in August, and by the return, at the end of the year, of those who had been detained in British prisons after the Rising. They included Eamonn de Valera, who rapidly rose to the top of the Sinn Fein organization.

British soldiers guarding an entrance to the Four Courts, one of Dublin's most important and outstanding buildings.

In 1917, five by-elections were held in Irish districts. Sinn Fein, which had not put up candidates since its failure at the polls in 1908, won every seat. In April, the United States entered the world war and increased its pressure on Britain to reach a fair settlement of the Irish problem. The new British prime minister, Lloyd George, summoned a convention in the hope of reaching such a settlement, but as both north and south still refused to consider a partition, the convention was a failure. The prestige of Sinn Fein, which had refused to have anything to do with Lloyd George's convention, rose still higher.

Meanwhile, the British government, frightened of another outbreak and particularly of a rising backed by the Germans, created anger and frustration with nit-picking regulations: no parades, no wearing of uniforms, arbitrary arrests. There was a tremendous public outcry when a prisoner on a hunger strike died after being forcibly fed.

The government in London made its crowning error in 1918 when it decided to enforce conscription in Ireland. The enormous casualties of World War I had already compelled the government to introduce compulsory military service in England, but the members of Redmond's party had made it plain as early as 1914 that they would never agree to its imposition in Ireland, and although Lloyd George promised to put home rule into effect at the same time as the draft, this concession cut no ice in Ireland. Opposition was solid, except, of course, in Ulster. Even the Irish

Above: Security check at the docks — barricade provided by Guinness brewery. Below: Internment — a surreptitious photograph of political prisoners in a prison camp somewhere in southern Ireland after the Rising.

bishops, generally a highly conservative body, issued a joint statement that "the Irish have a right to resist conscription by every means that are consonant with the laws of God."

Redmond and his colleagues opposed conscription just as strongly as Sinn Fein, and they withdrew from the British Parliament to help fight against it in Ireland. The authorities responded by arresting a number of Sinn Fein leaders while talking, not very convincingly, of a "German plot." Conscription would never have worked in Ireland, but, as it happened, the world war ended before it was put into effect.

Although the Home Rule party had wholeheartedly opposed it, conscription was probably the issue that finally destroyed the party, as the party under Redmond had become too closely associated with the British government. In the new atmosphere of militancy, the party seemed feeble and discredited. Immediately after the armistice, a general election was held. Before the election the Home Rule party — led by John Dillon after Redmond's sad death in March 1918 — held sixty-eight seats and Sinn Fein held three (although, of course, they refused to sit in them). After the election, Sinn Fein held seventy-three seats and the old Irish party held six — four of which had not been contested by Sinn Fein, to avoid splitting the vote and thereby letting in a Unionist.

War and Civil War

At the beginning of 1919, the Sinn Fein members formed their own Parliament of Ireland, or Dáil Éireann (the name still borne by the Irish Parliament), issued a declaration of independence, and formed a republican government with Eamonn de Valera as president. The British authorities were slow to suppress the republican government, but as they tried to maintain their grip on the country, more and more Sinn Fein leaders went to prison. Ireland slipped into war. It began with a few isolated acts of violence, but soon developed into large-scale guerrilla warfare, in which the British used irregular forces, including the notorious Black and Tans, as well as the police and regular army. Atrocities were committed on both sides. Liberal opinion in England revolted against the murders, burnings, and acts of reprisal that were carried out in the name of authority, and in December 1921, an agreement was finally reached between Lloyd George's government and an Irish delegation led by Arthur Griffith and Michael Collins, leader of the Irish Republican Army (IRA).

This agreement created the Irish Free State, which excluded the six northeastern counties of Ulster, and gave Ireland the status of a dominion, in which the king was acknowledged as head of the British commonwealth and a number of other concessions were made — such as the provision for British bases in Ireland. The treaty was thus a compromise and although it gave Ireland more freedom than the old home rule bill, it did not concede a fully independent republic.

The Free State treaty was not accepted by De Valera and other members of his government, although the Dáil approved it narrowly after a long and agonizing debate. De Valera and his associates resigned and Arthur Griffith became president. The position of Griffith's government was weak, and as the division between supporters and opponents of the treaty hardened, it became desperate. Civil war broke out, and once more Dublin echoed to the sound of gunfire. The conflict lasted for nearly a year, and by the time it ended, both Griffith and Michael Collins were dead. In May 1923, a truce was signed and the fighting ceased. But the bitterness lives on. Fifty years later, Ireland is still far from fulfilling the dreams of Connolly and Pearse.

Chronology

1800 – Act of Union (Great Britain and Ireland)

1845-49 – Great famine (heavy emigration begins)

1848 – "Young Ireland" insurrection

1867 – Fenian rebellion

1870 – Beginning of land reform

1886 – Defeat of Gladstone's first home rule bill

1891 – Fall of Parnell (split in Irish party)

1893 – Defeat of Gladstone's second home rule bill
       Gaelic League founded

1900 – Irish parliamentary party reunited under Redmond

1907 – First national convention of Sinn Fein

1908 – Defeat of Sinn Fein candidate in by-election
       Saint Enda's founded by Pearse

1910 – Connolly arrives in Ireland from United States

1912 – Third home rule bill introduced and passed

1913 – Dublin lock-out
       Larkin and Connolly found Irish Citizen Army
       MacNeill founds Irish Volunteers

1914 – Curragh Mutiny (April)
       Howth gun-running (July)
       World War I begins (August)
       Home rule passed but suspended (September)
       Split in Irish Volunteers (September)

1916

April 22 – Casement arrested; *Aud* scuttled

April 23 – MacNeill's countermanding order published

April 24 – The Rising begins

April 25 – Martial law proclaimed; British reinforcements begin
              to arrive
April 28 – Major-General Sir John Maxwell arrives in Ireland
April 29 – Pearse orders surrender
May   3 – Pearse, Clarke, MacDonagh shot
May   4 – Joseph Plunkett and three other leaders shot
May   5 – John MacBride shot
May   8 – Eamonn Ceannt, Michael Mallin, and two others shot
May   9 – Thomas Kent (of Fermoy) shot
May 11 – Dillon denounces executions; De Valera's sentence
              commuted
May 12 – Connolly, MacDermott shot
June   – Royal Commission of Inquiry censures Birrell
August – Casement executed

1917 – First Sinn Fein electoral victory (February)
       De Valera, Countess Markievicz released (June)
       De Valera elected as Sinn Fein candidate (July)
1918 – Attempt to introduce conscription (April)
       World War I armistice (November)
       General election; Sinn Fein win seventy-three seats (December)
1919 – Sinn Fein sets up Dáil Éireann; open revolt (January)
1921 – Irish Free State treaty

A Note on Further Reading

Although modern Irish history has not been so thoroughly researched as (for instance) modern American history, there are a great many books on the subject. The list below is only intended as a guide to further reading and as an acknowledgment of some works that have been useful in writing this book.

Among general histories, the best is probably F. S. L. Lyons, *Ireland Since the Famine* (1971). P. S. O Hegarty, *History of Ireland under the Union 1801–1922* (1952) is the work of a man who himself made a contribution to Irish history, both before and after the Rising. Edward Norman, *A History of Modern Ireland* (1971) is less favorable to the Irish than most of the books listed here.

Of the Rising itself, perhaps the best account is still Desmond Ryan, *The Rising* (1949, 3d ed., 1957); the author was a pupil at Saint Enda's and was with Pearse at the G.P.O. Max Caulfield, *The Easter Rebellion* (1964) is exciting if perhaps rather imaginative in places. So is Thomas M. Coffey, *Agony at Easter* (1969). Edgar Holt, *Protest in Arms: The Irish Troubles 1916–23* (1964) covers that difficult period clearly.

The following books contain material on different aspects of the Rising:

Owen Dudley Edwards and Fergus Pyle, eds., *1916 — The Easter Rising* (1968)

K. B. Nowlan, ed., *The Making of 1916* (1969)

F. X. Martin, ed., *Leaders and Men of the Easter Rising* (1967)

C. C. O'Brien, ed., *The Shaping of Modern Ireland 1891–1916* (1960)

Desmond Williams, ed., *The Irish Struggle 1916–26* (1966)

Of many eyewitness accounts, James Stephens, *The Insurrection in Dublin* (1916, 3d ed., 1965) is by a sympathetic neutral; *The Memoirs of Desmond Fitzgerald* (1968) is by a participant. The *Report* of the Royal Commission on the Rebellion in Ireland (1916) makes interesting reading, and the British view of events in Dublin is described by Leon O Broin in *Dublin Castle and the 1916 Rising* (1966) and *The Chief Secretary: Augustine Birrell in Ireland* (1969). Other useful biographies are:

Desmond Greaves, *Life and Times of James Connolly* (1961)

Denis Gwynn, *John Redmond* (1932)

L. N. Le Roux, *Tom Clarke and the Irish Freedom Movement* (1936)

Lord Longford and T. P. O'Neill, *Eamonn de Valera* (1970)

Desmond Ryan, *Patrick Pearse* (1919)

The influence of Irish-American opinion is described in A. J. Ward, *Ireland and Anglo-American Relations 1899–1921* (1969).

Index

About the Author

Late in the 1960's, Neil Grant gave up his career as a full-time encyclopedia editor and part-time writer in New York City and returned to his native England to devote all of his energies to creating books for young people. Before going to the United States to work — first as a teacher — Mr. Grant had been a student (he holds a master's degree from Cambridge University). In addition to *The Easter Rising*, Franklin Watts, Inc., has published the following books by Mr. Grant: *Benjamin Disraeli, Charles V, Victoria: Queen and Empress, The Renaissance* (A First Book), *Munich: 1938, Cathedrals* (A First Book), and *Guilds* (A First Book).